VALENTINE PLACE

❧

POEMS

DAVID LEHMAN

SCRIBNER PAPERBACK POETRY
NEW YORK LONDON TORONTO SYDNEY TOKYO SINGAPORE

SCRIBNER PAPERBACK POETRY
1230 Avenue of the Americas
New York, NY 10020

SCRIBNER PAPERBACK POETRY and design are trademarks of Simon & Schuster Inc.

DESIGNED BY ERICH HOBBING

Manufactured in the United States of America

1   3   5   7   9   10   8   6   4   2

Library of Congress Cataloging-in-Publication Data
Lehman, David, date.
Valentine place: poems / David Lehman.
p.   cm.
I. Title.
PS3562.E428V35   1995
811'.54—dc20   95-38090
CIP

ISBN 0-684-82279-2

In the noon and the afternoon of life we still throb at the recollection of days when happiness was not happy enough, but must be drugged with the relish of pain and fear; for he touched the secret of the matter who said of love—

"All other pleasures are not worth its pains":

and when the day was not long enough, but the night too must be consumed in keen recollections; when the head boiled all night on the pillow with the generous deed it resolved on; when the moonlight was a pleasing fever and the stars were letters and the flowers ciphers and the air was coined into song; when all business seemed an impertinence, and all the men and women running to and fro in the streets, mere pictures.

RALPH WALDO EMERSON, "Love"

CONTENTS

❦

PART III
VALENTINE PLACE

PART IV

VALENTINE PLACE

WEDDING SONG

❦

Poetry is a criticism of life
As a jailbreak is a criticism of prison.
I now pronounce you man and wife.

The pencil has no chance against the knife,
You can't compete with television.
Poetry used to be a criticism of life.

Because you play together like a drum and fife
On the Fourth of July, your favorite season,
I now pronounce you man and wife.

The sonnets resisted, though they were rife
With clues subjected to a critic's misprision:
Poetry may not be a criticism of life.

In a field full of purple loosestrife,
Does happiness require a reason?
I now pronounce you man and wife.

The fruits of peace, to be peeled with a knife,
Await your teeth. It's your decision.
Is poetry a criticism of life?
I now pronounce you man and wife.

PART I

THE CHOICE

He had to choose. He could fight the Vietnam war
In a helicopter rescuing diplomats from Saigon
In his dreams or in the icy silence of the tomb
He and his wife had been living in since April—

Or he could refuse in favor of a love affair
With a woman who swam the English Channel
Using two strokes. She had high cheekbones and jet-black hair,
Or maybe it was foxy eyes and a mop of brown curls.
Anyway she had infiltrated his dreams.
He lowered his voice. "War and peace may be great themes,"
He said, "but adultery is even greater."

It was their last conversation in bed.
"You're going to miss me," she said,
"Kiss me," he heard,
And the prediction began to come true
With her voice still in his ear.

"Sometimes what you thought was an interruption
Turns out to be your life.
And sometimes what you thought was your life
Turns out to have been an interruption.
And yet you have to act
As if you were back in the fourth grade
And knew the right answer was Pittsburgh
But put down Bethlehem just to see what would happen—
How it would feel to be wrong."

DAVID LEHMAN

❧

Some people find out they are Jews.
They can't believe it.
They had always hated Jews.
As children they had roamed in gangs on winter nights in the old
neighborhood, looking for Jews.
They were not Jewish, they were Irish.
They brandished broken bottles, tough guys with blood on their
lips, looking for Jews.
They intercepted Jewish boys walking alone and beat them up.
Sometimes they were content to chase the Jew and he could elude
them by running away. They were happy just to see him run
away. The coward! All Jews were yellow.
They spelled Jew with a small j jew.
And now they find out they are Jews themselves.
It happened at the time of the Spanish Inquisition.
To escape persecution, they pretended to convert to Christianity.
They came to this country and settled in the Southwest.
At some point the oral tradition failed the family, and their
secret faith died.
No one would ever have known if not for the bones that turned up
on the dig.
A disaster. How could it have happened to them?
They are in a state of panic—at first.
Then they realize that it is the answer to their prayers.
They hasten to the synagogue or build new ones.
They are Jews at last!
They are free to marry other Jews, and divorce them, and intermarry
with Gentiles, God forbid.
They are model citizens, clever and thrifty.
They debate the issues.

They fire off earnest letters to the editor.

They vote.

They are resented for being clever and thrifty.

They buy houses in the suburbs and agree not to talk so loud.

They look like everyone else, drive the same cars as everyone else,
      yet in their hearts they know they're different.

In every *minyan* there are always two or three, hated by the others,
      who give life to one ugly stereotype or another:

The grasping Jew with the hooked nose or the Ivy League Bolshevik
      who thinks he is the agent of world history.

But most of them are neither ostentatiously pious nor excessively
      avaricious.

How I envy them! They *believe*.

How I envy them their annual family reunion on Passover,
      anniversary of the Exodus, when all the uncles and aunts and
      cousins get together.

They wonder about the heritage of Judaism they are passing along
      to their children.

Have they done as much as they could to keep the old embers
      burning?

Others lead more dramatic lives.

A few go to Israel.

One of them calls Israel "the ultimate concentration camp."

He tells Jewish jokes.

On the plane he gets tipsy, tries to seduce the stewardess.

People in the Midwest keep telling him he reminds them of Woody
      Allen.

He wonders what that means. I'm funny? A sort of nervous
      intellectual type from New York? A Jew?

Around this time somebody accuses him of not being Jewish enough.

It is said by resentful colleagues that his parents changed their
      name from something that sounded more Jewish.

Everything he publishes is scrutinized with reference to "the
      Jewish question."

It is no longer clear what is meant by that phrase.

He has already forgotten all the Yiddish he used to know, and the
people of that era are dying out one after another.
The number of witnesses keeps diminishing.
Soon there will be no one left to remind the others and their
children.
That is why he came to this dry place where the bones have come to
life.
To live in a state of perpetual war puts a tremendous burden on the
population. As a visitor he felt he had to share that burden.
With his gift for codes and ciphers, he joined the counter-
terrorism unit of army intelligence.
Contrary to what the spook novels say, he found it possible to
avoid betraying either his country or his lover.
This was the life: strange bedrooms, the perfume of other men's
wives.
As a spy he had a unique mission: to get his name on the front page
of the nation's newspaper of record. Only by doing that would
he get the message through to his immediate superior.
If he goes to jail, he will do so proudly; if they're going to hang
him anyway, he'll do something worth hanging for.
In time he may get used to being the center of attention, but this
was incredible:
To talk his way into being the chief suspect in the most flamboyant
murder case in years!
And he was innocent!
He could prove it!
And what a book he would write when they free him from this prison:
A novel, obliquely autobiographical, set in Vienna in the twilight
of the Hapsburg Empire, in the year that his mother was born.

DARK PASSAGE

❧

He said he missed the city. He meant he missed her
And her habit of bumming cigarettes, showing up late,
Looking rich. It was no wonder he couldn't remember
Her face in the morning, or the name of the country
He was in, or the exact nature of his mission. He was
Afraid that if he looked at her, he'd lose her, but
He couldn't help himself. And she looked back
With the largest saddest eyes he had ever seen.
Then she was gone, swallowed by an oceanic crowd,
A Mardi Gras crowd full of pickpockets and thieves,
And the distance between the lovers kept widening,
And he kept calling her name. The ocean spewed her out
On a foreign shore. Some people wore masks.
Everyone had drunk too much wine. It was dark,
And the tape in the bistro lasted sixty minutes,
So he had now heard "These Foolish Things" in French
Seven times, only this time someone else was with him,
Whose face he never gets to see. Sleep this once
Came speedily. His ambition was lofty.
She said she meant him. She really meant anyone.

THE SECRET LIFE

She was strange. Even as a child she had been able
To picture her own death, as a prisoner pictures freedom.
The first time they met, he walked her to her third-floor walkup
On a city landmark block, tiny but with a lot of light.

The first time they went to bed, Mahler's Fourth Symphony
Was on the record player. They traded insults, had a fight
To juice themselves up for the main event, and in the morning,
Her guilt and his anger were gone. Neither of them could remember

The reason for the delay: hadn't their analysts explained
The loss of his wallet, her keys, that weekend at the shore?
The last time they went to bed, both of them knew it;

The neighbors knew it in the morning when her mother came
To collect her things, and her father mentioned his lawyer.
He felt like a burglar in his own living room when they left.

It started in the subway in Boston, where he thought he saw her
Before he knew who she was. The Red Sox were scheduled to play
Oakland that night at Fenway, but it rained all day
And he went to see a Hitchcock double feature instead.

He met her there, in the second half of *Vertigo*
And the first half of *Rear Window*. Afterwards they walked.
Neither of them was hungry, and both of them
Had something they wanted to keep quiet about.

He kept comparing Grace Kelly and Kim Novak in his mind,
Wondering about the woman he was with, and how little
He knew about her. Was it enough to get him to follow her

Into the Spanish church with the high tower
Where he was sure to have a dizzy spell
At dusk, after he rescued her from drowning?

Every time she left him she took off her wedding ring,
Slammed it on the dresser top, stormed out. Four hours later,
Sex was better than ever. They stayed up late to watch
The debonair husband bring his fragile wife a glass of milk.

Had he put poison in it? Or was it just his wife's bad nerves?
Clearly, *he* got on hers. She said he was too contentious.
They could never just enjoy a movie like ordinary people,
They had to analyze it to death. One day she locked herself

In the bathroom, sobbing, saying she had taken a lethal dose
Of Dalmane. It wasn't true, but he believed her, and made her drink
The vile stuff prescribed by the emergency-room guy on the phone.

She was scared of him, and basked in the fear, egging him on
To see him lose his temper while she kept cool and sarcastic,
Playing the role of the bitch, knowing how much he liked it.

As phone sex is to sex, so was their strained dialogue
To the quarrel they should have had. He brought up the baby.
All she could think of was the casserole in the oven.
She rehearsed the day's doings: X made a pass at her, Y frowned

When he said good morning, and Z is up a creek because
Her boyfriend has AIDS. He listened with one ear tuned

DAVID LEHMAN

21

To the Mets game on the radio, down six to four in the eighth
But with the bases loaded and HoJo at the plate. Ball one.

He kept turning over sentences in his mind: "Her husband
Never suspected, not because he was dense but because
It hadn't occurred to him that other men might desire her

As he did not." And, "Maybe she needed to treat herself
To a breakdown, or maybe just a glass of water and a pill."
Every time he left her, he phoned her two weeks after.

Should she listen to his shrink sessions on tape, which
He had left behind—deliberately, she supposed?
Her shrink would have called it "an accident with intent,"
On the grounds that there were no accidents, no errors,

No false prophets or dreams, no mistakes that weren't messages
From the unconscious, texts for her to interpret and complete.
The tapes were meant for her ears only. Love abolished ethics:
That was her philosophy, and she would take it into the street

And see what happened. The prospect exhilarated her. Here at last
Was a project commensurate with her energy, her fanatical zeal
To do good works and get her hands dirty, be among the people,

Until she heard his voice on tape, going on and on about his moral
Dilemmas. His feelings had changed. He didn't want to hurt hers.
All this talk about feelings. . . . She wanted to slug him.

He brought up the baby, which was strange because
They didn't have a baby. She tried to reason with him, but
Humoring him was smarter. He was mixed up. One drink too many,
An extra toke of exceptional grass. No appetite, no sleep.

His lawyer explained how he could cheat her. He got indignant.
"I don't want to cheat her," he said. His lawyer sighed,
"It's your funeral." His favorite expression.
The object of the game was to make the ball disappear.

They checked in. He asked for a double room
With a king-sized bed. "You're very sure of yourself,"
She said, when the clerk went to get the key.

Raindrops in the sun, on the windshield, on the roses,
Blackening their crimson; on her cheek, a tear; in the air,
The trace of her giveaway smile in the getaway car.

She used to visit him before he knew who she was,
What she looked like, and why she came to him
At night, when the others were asleep. And now . . .
Was it possible? Was she the same woman

Framed in the window's tall landscape
Of pine trees receiving the evening's blue powder?
He had thrown away the frame, wanting her to enter the picture,
And he would go there with her, down country lanes

In France, where the pears were ripening
In poems of pleasure that had not yet been written,
For he could imagine an embrace as fierce as the one she fled from,

As cold as the taste of snow on burning lips,
And was prepared to love her in a shabby unlighted corner
Of the attic, on the shortest day of the year.

DAVID LEHMAN

BREEZE MARINE

La chair est triste, hélas! et j'ai lu tous les livres.
MALLARMÉ, "Brise Marine"

The impeccable old man, who chaired the committee,
Reported a vague but pervasive sadness
In the land, causing the people who lived by the sea
To stare at the sea for hours, with their backs to the land,
Inhaling deeply, dreaming of platters of oysters and clams.
The boy nodded. He knew that patriotism was just
A craving for food loved as a boy in Rockaway Beach.

The boy was disappointed with the sins of the flesh,
The sadness after sex.
Not guilt, though sometimes that, too, entered into it,
But a sort of dazed surprise to find where lust had led him.

The man said:
"O what a magnificent invention was the Id
Freud fashioned out of the dreams and errors
Of turn-of-the-century neurotics in Vienna,
The city where Hitler grew up, wanting to become a painter."

"But that does not explain the sadness, or invalidate it,"
The boy replied.

The man looked at the boy and said:
"Although you may read many books, so many
You imagine you have read them all,

There will always be one more on the shelf above your bed
You will not be able to finish before falling asleep.
Remember: to escape into a novel about French decadence
Is as good as escaping via a seaworthy vessel
Headed for mutiny in the South Seas.
If there's anything the nineteenth century taught us, it's that."

The boy put his sandals on his head, turned around,
And walked away without a sound.

This is what he thought:

"Evil tears. Sad flesh. Paper void.
The moment of grace was when
The misfit held a gun to the old woman's temple.
In this place, prayer is the howl of a dog,
The rabbi strangled with his own prayer shawl.
The last words he heard were, 'Kill the Jew.'
That was how he knew that God was watching.

"I will never forget that moment.
The wailing was terrible, the sirens unbearable.

"Anyway the hero turns around at this point
As the true dimensions of the catastrophe dawn on him
At last. There is a pink glow in the distance,
Faint; a whiff of salt in his nostrils. He sees
Handkerchiefs waved by ladies in white dresses.
He hears the horns of departure. Nothing can stop him now!"

Picking up the pen he sat for a moment
Daunted by the whiteness of the page. It was like
Snow in college lawns before footprints deface it.
Those footprints were going to be his,

Even now he could picture the path, leading to the past,
A particular June morning, a tryst in Hellas,
White waves, cries of gulls. The bunch of grapes.
An instant, and it was gone. The place was
The place he'd dreamed about in his dreams of escape.

SEXISM

The happiest moment in a woman's life
Is when she hears the turn of her lover's key
In the lock, and pretends to be asleep
When he enters the room, trying to be
Quiet but clumsy, bumping into things,
And she can smell the liquor on his breath
But forgives him because she has him back
And doesn't have to sleep alone.

The happiest moment in a man's life
Is when he climbs out of bed
With a woman, after an hour's sleep,
After making love, and pulls on
His trousers, and walks outside,
And pees in the bushes, and sees
The high August sky full of stars
And gets in his car and drives home.

THE VISIT

❧

One night at a bar his old college buddy Allen
Had two things to say. He was getting a divorce
From Marcia, twenty years his wife. Also, he was gay.
He stank of drink, was sentimental, felt old.
In the elevator he quizzed the others about *their* divorces,
The formulas they used to divide their common property
And other things better left unsaid in front of strangers,
Including the stranger he married. And away he went
In the first cab that came, which turned into a police car
With its siren switched on the moment Allen stepped inside
And left his youth behind, standing under a street lamp.
It was a pleasure to be rid of the pest, a pleasure to be
Alone in the brisk November night, walking past shop windows
Reflecting the shocked look of the man in the mirror,
A pleasure to think of the woman waiting for him upstairs.
In fact, it was incredible: the traumas of the past
From which he thought he would never awaken
Had simply casually faded away, like a receding siren,
And the only thing visible in the blank darkness
Was the outline of her smile, that woman seen once
And fleetingly, leaving a crowded skyscraper elevator,
An image without a body. And the life she would have led
If she had disappeared—if she hadn't married him.

STAGES ON LIFE'S WAY

❧

1. The Night Before

He liked waiting. Waiting gave him a purpose to live.
Waiting outside the marriage counselor's office,
He read that the unconscious is structured like a language.
The verbs in the dream he had the night before were

Copulating on flying carpets or chasing taxis in Tokyo,
Always doing something, taking action, not just waiting
As he was doing now, waiting quietly in an armchair holding a book,
Or pacing back and forth like an expectant husband,

Waiting for the appointment with the insignificant clerk
Without whose signature the elopement would be canceled,
Waiting without anxiety, knowing that the time of the wait

Would be infinite and how much clear thinking could be done,
Waiting for the dinner bell, for the music to begin,
Waiting for the fog to lift, so the darkness could be seen.

2. The Morning After

"You're a bastard," she said,
Admiringly. He was; he admitted it. He saved his own book
From the flames, letting hers burn. How young he looked!
She spat: "I'd rather be dead."

The ritual began with a kiss, as it always did.
The one-armed man identified himself. "My name," he flashed

His teeth, "is death." And the fruit in her mouth turned to ash
In the darkened hotel room, under the coverlet.

A ringing phone interrupted their embrace.
She put a hand to her face.
Where had he seen her before? In somebody else's window.

The woman in the painting was somebody else's widow,
Somebody else's wife.
But that was art, and this was life.

3. THE NEXT DAY

He was impulsive. One day he decided to read Conrad
And bought *The Secret Agent*, *Victory*, and *Under Western Eyes*.
The next day he had a craving for canned fruits
And came home with purple plums in heavy syrup, Queen Anne
     cherries

In light syrup, and pineapple chunks in juice, no sugar added.
Also, he wasn't going to the theater enough, so he lined up seats
For *Gypsy* and *City of Angels*. Then he forgot to go, and left
The cans of fruit in the icebox, and put Conrad on the shelf.

The next disaster hadn't yet begun. So there was time
To find out what she was like as a child, and they could be
Children together in her parents' hotel room, opening the drawers,

Hiding in the closet, and she put on her mother's pearl necklace,
And later they looked for snakes behind bushes, and she fell down.
It was summer: a bowl of ripe apricots, the mud on their knees.

THE INTERRUPTION

❦

The little details defeated him.
There was always something in the way, something to be done.
He would never arrive. A stone would block the entrance
To the cave where he was supposed to go, to study or to pray.
He would never have even left the house. A ringing phone
Would have made him think twice about the scheme his brother
The broker concocted to cut his taxes in half for '91,
But at just that moment his nostrils detected smoke in the bedroom
And a decision was postponed until the next interruption.
It was maddening. The moment he made up his mind to act,
A fresh emergency would distract him.
Nor do we ever find out what happened next—whether the stone
In the cave mouth gave way, the broker's scheme
Led to lawsuits and heartbreak, and the house burned down.
Each digression was like a fresh transgression
And nothing is more liberating than sin
When the hero's feet leave the ground and something stronger
Than faith interrupts the pull of gravity.
A fly interrupts his reverie. How hard it was to concentrate,
To keep his mind on just one thing, when that thing
Was changing as he was looking, and a phone was ringing
In the background. There was no time for the contemplative life
He had once thought he wanted. He had to catch it on the fly,
Like reflections in the blackened windows of a train
Pulling out of the station, with his parents waving goodbye
From the last car while he ran the length of the platform, crying,
"Don't go. Don't leave me alone. Please interrupt this nightmare
With a daydream about a little boy who wanted a dog
Or, failing that, a younger brother." His analyst
Interrupts him: "Time's up." Meanwhile the train is stuck

Between two stations, but he's not on it. In fact,
He can't leave the house, can't even get down the stairs.
In the attic, where he went to be alone,
He could see the tops of the tall pines
Shivering in the breeze, and pictured
The rest of the garden, with thick brush strokes.
Sitting transfixed in front of the attic window,
He invented the landscape, filled it with birdsong,
And savored the cries of children walking home from school,
Heard from a distance in the mild March afternoon—
Until a boy with bloodied knees turns up in the back door
And the next interruption has begun.

PART II

THE PUBLIC SECTOR

❧

1.

From the point of view of a man
With a wife and a child and a job, who knows
The resistance of material things,
Deadlines and coffee stains and an irate boss,
Life is a public event, and childhood
Was when our lives were private
And we were scared of growing up because

We knew it would be the end of us. It was
The same fear we had felt in Madrid, standing
In the Valley of the Fallen
Before heading for a café, where we drank beer
And ate mussels with hot sauce and lemon.
For a minute we could smell it:
Bad red wine, strong perfume, the threat of violence.

There was also a third possibility:
That this was a story of man's love and woman's anger,
Not the fall of darkness but its lasting vastness,
The father's return from the dead to chide his son
For taking too long, doing too little. The summer leaks away.
I captured a cricket in a soda glass
And let it go, saving the music for a January day.

DAVID LEHMAN

2.

But that was in another country, and besides,
The wench is still alive, beside me here in bed.
The vastness of the darkness was what attracted me to it,
And the curve of space. It was as if the sky were a bowl
And we stood upside down in a concave mirror
The size of a soup spoon, surrounded by stars.
The sunsets were glorious. A slender pine tree,

Blue clouds, white sky, a streak of orange light.
Pleasant evening breezes. I decided that I was happiest then,
Hungriest then, before the opposition
Of private desire and public duty
Became a tiresome cliché. Our days were committed
To pleasure and a theory of pleasure
As if life were an event that could be judged

Solely on esthetic grounds. While you slept, I walked,
Tossed pebbles across a brook and watched
The ripples widen and intersect. Thus I learned
The names of the flowers—not to master them
But to know their secrets, because poetry is naming
And calling, recalling the names
Months later, in the cold quick autumn dusk.

3.

History was a dream of the future
Which you tried to remember but couldn't because
You forgot to write it down. Writing is memory,
But poetry is also the rejection of memory if
To forget is divine. It was spring in the city

When I was a boy and the fall of night meant
The end of freedom. The fall of one god meant the fall

Of all: knowledge that absolved us of nothing.
In the city, all lives are public. It's like
Unedited footage, unrehearsed, seemingly random
And generated by reckless energy. You can't get
Enough of it. The city itself is like a drug,
A wonder drug. It makes the addict think
He has found the fountain of youth.

There was also a third possibility:
That this was the story of a man on a train
To whom nothing out of the ordinary will happen.
All the men and women he meets
Are enigmatic, ambivalent, self-conscious, hesitant
Yet bold enough to knock down the ladder
After using it to reach the roof, where they are,

4.

In public view, for strangers to read about
In newspapers the next day. The celebration of vertigo
By people who are afraid of heights
Is entered into evidence here, as is the testimony
Of witnesses who saw the defendant
Edging to the rim of the continent,
Where the abyss begins. I went to a convention

Of professors and heard a philosopher say
It was possible to earn a salary in the high five figures
And maintain your ability to creep to the edge
Of the abyss. It was entertaining to watch

But the melancholy of the observer soon set in
And the mystery of departure, as the spray hits the deck,
And the women at the port wave goodbye.

It's a question *of* as well as *for* the imagination:
You look at the sky and wonder about the powers
We have granted to the heavens, the old gods that fell
And the stars that surround us, the stars beyond number
We praise in poems because of the distance they travel
And their light, however faint, which makes them
Beloved of us who love the darkness as we do.

THE DROWNING

My mother told me the story, and I believed it:
About the boy who went out too far,
Beyond the voices of older sister and smarter brother,
Exhausted father smoking a cigar and reading the paper,
Distracted mother changing the baby's diaper:
He left them behind and walked into the sea
And vanished in the foam and never came back.
And I promised that I wouldn't do what he did
But I wanted to know more about him, and vowed
To bring him back to life, and my mother laughed.

And I am still that boy standing on the shore
Alone, abandoned by his grown-up brother, or
Stranded with the woman that he married
And their ill-tempered brood, with sand in their hair,
As the waves advance, the spray hits the air
Like snow falling upwards, and nothing will bring him back,
The red-haired boy who commanded the waves,
With a conductor's wand, before he disappeared in the sea,
In the story my mother told so well that even though
She made it up I was sure it had happened to me.

1967

❦

In the year 1867 Thomas Hardy wrote a poem called "1967," in which he remarks that the best thing he can say about that year is the fact that he is not going to live to see it.

NORTHROP FRYE, *The Modern Century* (1967)

The geniuses of the revolution were upstairs, plotting.
The war was everywhere. The war was a mass-produced fiction.
The girl played Antigone and showed me her breasts.
I dreamed of her nude on horseback, her long blond curls
Flowing behind her, like Dürer's Eve. I wrote a sestina,
My first, about her. The poem's six repeating end-words
Were *coffee, grass, speed, fuck, war*, and *revolution*.

Marlboro was merely a stage on the road to Camels.
The theory was, no theory was needed, just action. Revolution
Wasn't yet the rock song they played while the basketball players
Had their pre-game practice. The war was elsewhere. The war was
On the blackboard where the initials "C.I." stood for
Categorical Imperative at nine o'clock and Color Index seven
Hours later. I said "I want you" and she said "I know."

Seven hours was the average length of a mescaline trip,
Though you still felt high the next day. Somebody
Got punched out in the subway, and I took out my notebook
And wrote, "The war is over." A brainstorm. The dead bodies on TV
Were somebody's paranoid fantasy. The girl said nothing.
She had dark hair and no name. I told Leslie I had a new girlfriend
And he looked at me coolly and said, "Is she beautiful?"

The girl had a dark beauty mark on her left cheek.
Her motto was: "Reject everything, regret nothing."
The grass was adequate; a forest-green V-neck sweater on the bed
Became a meadow in the afternoon. Everything was possible:
You could have Christmas on earth just by printing a few good
Dirty jokes, spur-of-the-moment poems, a recipe for hash
Brownies. Thus the Xerox machine had revolutionized our lives.

The girl said something's wrong. Her periods, feeble to begin with,
Had stopped and yet she wasn't pregnant. She sure knew how
To scare a guy. She was the main character in my poems, the one
Who told me she could never love me. Then she came to my room,
And let me take off her forest-green V-neck sweater.
The war came later. For the sake of the revolution she posed
As Liberty at the barricades of Delacroix's picture.

Coffee was "slow" speed and I was always hungry,
Always moving, putting off the moment of going to bed
Until dawn. Then the girl did her Salome dance for me alone.
I told Leslie I was in love with her and he said
All that meant was I wanted a blow job from a stranger
While reading the newspaper, for I was the American male
And that's what the American male wants. (Leslie was British,

A photographer, who waited until we graduated
To tell me he was gay.) The revolution was everywhere
That summer—you could see it in a black-and-white photograph
Of dawn, later captioned a sunset by mistake
In the newsroom. Though the war was confined
To the family's living room, the revolution was never far away.
You could feel it on the streets, in the rain, after dark.

You could smell it in the coffee, see it swirling
Like fragments of cream swirling in a mug of espresso,

Which we discovered that fall. The revolution required
It, and poetry. The revolution demanded greener grass,
A new girlfriend. Candor as never before. Bloodshed
As never imagined. Getting arrested with her in Central Park,
At an anti-war rally, the day after the first night we fucked.

ON THE NATURE OF DESIRE

❦

1.

There are, said my old philosophy professor, two kinds
Of people in the world: those who divide everything in two
And those who don't. At the dinner party, Janice was talking

About computers. IBMs are masculine, she said. Macintoshes
Are feminine. That's exactly what some people say
About art and nature, said her husband, Ben. Do you really

Believe that, asked Mark. I mean, should hurricanes be named
After women, as in the old days, and is the construction of a city
The quintessential male act, Nature subdued by Apollo's merry men?

2.

Nature, then, is the great eruption—flood, earthquake,
Tidal wave, volcano—that interrupts the World Series
And sends men running to their cars and their private visions

Of sublime waterfalls in the early nineteenth century when
Man could feel alone in a benevolent universe whose god
Was not an almighty moralist but the outburst of an imagination

Capable of anything. Nature is the calamity that overwhelms man
With terror yet draws him into it, and he creeps to the edge
Of the canyon, holding the hand of the woman he loves.

DAVID LEHMAN

3.

The laws governing isosceles triangles do not apply
To man, wife, and child. The professor of mathematics is one
Of two men in love with the same woman. The other is his son

By a previous mistress. Both are fearless.
They know that Nature is a woman, a forest on fire
That can't stop burning. The goal is not to quench the fire

But to let it burn. The dancing around the fire goes on
All night, and the victorious couple is the last
To drop down exhausted and consummate their love.

4.

I saw her again this evening. She had the face of the woman
With the braided hair at the desk in the public library,
Where she used to work before she grew up and I moved away.

When I got up close I could tell how young she was—maybe seventeen,
The age we were when we met. I was reading *The Sun Also Rises*
And she walked over, brought me a pile of books about Hemingway,

And let her hand linger on mine, accidentally brushed.
Neither of us understood the nature of our desire,
Just that it was mutual. Our ignorance fed the fire.

5.

In those days you could have a girl in your dormitory room
Twice a month, on Saturday night, from seven in the evening
Until one A.M. The lights were out, but the dust of my window

Caught the glare of a street lamp and the reflection of a neon
"Chop Suey" sign. An imaginary wind lifted her skirt,
And she smiled, letting me look. "You know, you could be expelled

For this." She had theories: she was Catholic, I was Jewish.
She was ashamed of her breasts, I was proud of my poems.
The antitheses were alluring in the early morning light.

6.

There are those who insist that all differences except
The biological are trivial and that the oppositions
Between Apollo and Dionysus, nature and culture and so on,

Are all of them sentimental and false, because they concern
Only the man and the woman, neglecting the third who walks always
Beside them. The great mystery is time and how we lost it

And cannot get it back, cannot convert memory into action,
The slim-breasted girl in the public library; can barely recall
The face in the photograph, the body beneath my own.

7.

Man in the state of nature was unalienated from his labor
Or in a state of constant warfare with his fellow primates.
They fought over an ordinary woman in an ordinary bar,

As if the fear of death didn't matter. The survivor wins her.
She is convinced he has put her on a pedestal in order
To look up her skirt: once a philosopher, twice a pervert.

DAVID LEHMAN

Watching the couple's antics in bed are his mother and father,
Her mother and father, and the Marquis de Sade.
The son, asleep in the next room, is guarded by angels.

8.

In summer camp, the girl knows that any partner,
However unappealing, is better than no partner at all,
So she agrees to dance with him, a slow dance, an awkward waltz,

And when the torture is over, and their bodies separate,
He is shocked at what he sees: "Your dress is bleeding."
The boy becomes a man when his desire distracts him

From his fear, and he cannot resist the return to her womb
Though it rhymes with death at every orifice. The dress
Is put on to be taken off, the bed made to be undone.

9.

Why, then, is this city full of randy men, anxious
To cheat on their wives, and lonely women, who learned to say no
To importunate suitors long ago? If the scholars of sex

Are right, every Eve defends herself against her own desire
While trying to allay Adam's fear. If the poets of sex
Are right, the exchange of body fluids is a function

Of natural thirst, and love is the speechless joy
That lasts until it dies, and the couple close their eyes,
Tired, unashamed, nude and asleep for their hour together.

UNDER THE INFLUENCE

❧

The antithetical sense of primal rhymes, like "womb" and "tomb,"
Charmed me at times. My favorite hour was twilight gloom:
The influence of a Parma violet in a sinister hospital room.

The influence of the Hermit on the Lovers and the Star
Came later, when I graduated from Columbia, and at the West End Bar
Discussed the influence of a clubfoot on Lord Byron's "stance."

The difference between prose and verse, the walk and the dance,
Was next. I thought I understood
The influence of infancy on the car keys of adulthood.

The difference between olives and onions in gin and vermouth
Came closer to the truth
When I worked at the budget bureau in a sort of trance—

And how gold in Germany differs from silver in France.
I contemplated the nature of a terrestrial heaven
Thanks to the puzzling influence of insomnia at twenty-seven,

Which led me to the opera on alternate Tuesday nights,
To the theater on Wednesdays, and Fridays to the fights
In smoke-filled arenas nearby. Don't ask why

The difference between spruces in January and maples in July
Now seems crucial. Yesterday the influence of white on green:
Tomorrow the difference between the erotic and the obscene.

The significance, too, of movies and Broadway tunes
On evenings influenced by aching athletic afternoons
And the difference a day makes, by the light of the moon.

DAVID LEHMAN

THE WORLD TRADE CENTER

❧

I never liked the World Trade Center.
When it went up I talked it down
As did many other New Yorkers.
The twin towers were ugly monoliths
That lacked the details the ornament the character
Of the Empire State Building and especially
The Chrysler Building, everyone's favorite,
With its scalloped top, so noble.
The World Trade Center was an example of what was wrong
With American architecture,
And it stayed that way for twenty-five years
Until that Friday afternoon in February
When the bomb went off and the buildings became
A great symbol of America, like the Statue
Of Liberty at the end of Hitchcock's *Saboteur*.
My whole attitude toward the World Trade Center
Changed overnight. I began to like the way
It comes into view as you reach Sixth Avenue
From any side street, the way the tops
Of the towers dissolve into white skies
In the east when you cross the Hudson
Into the city across the George Washington Bridge.

THE ROLE MODEL

୧✦୨

With the lawyer in the three-piece suit, she was frigid.
With the dungaree-clad sculptor, who assembles his pieces
Out of bumpers and tires picked up at a car graveyard,
She has multiple orgasms. I can smell the popcorn.
You can tell what's going to happen. It's everyone's fault:
Grandfather for bossing grandmother around, the lawyer
For being a Wasp wearing a bowtie, the first husband
For being anal retentive, and the first husband's
Second wife for being invisible. But she doesn't get to keep
The baby, who is now seven years old. She can't be a mother
And have sex, or she can't have sex and like it. This is what
The movie is saying over and over and over. For sex
You have to go elsewhere, leave Boston behind, go to a bar
Near Lincoln Center and wear tight dresses. If she runs
A fashionable shoe store in Midtown, she will be accused
Of murder, because she happened to answer the personals
And lay a few guys. Either sex means danger, or danger means
Good sex. (Luckily her mother is living with her to baby-sit
The child.) Some women are still unmotivated, still liable
To run off at a moment's notice to find out who they are,
Leaving the baby, a second-grade boy this time, in the care
Of manic dad, who is about to lose his job on Madison Avenue.
She can't have sex *or* the child; she has to have her career
And her midlife crisis. Much is made of her salary, bigger
Than his, and that is important to her, but so is sex,
And how come she isn't getting any? Are all men married
Or gay? She doesn't know the answer to that question,
But she's smart, cholesterol-conscious, knows how to change
The oil in her car, and has a wide wardrobe of possibilities

DAVID LEHMAN
49

To choose from. She has read the magazines, and that doesn't mean
Harper's Bazaar in the Village apartment of her fiancé,
The voyeur photographer, while he snores away, leg in a cast,
And she wonders if he will propose to her when he wakes up.

PARABLE

❧

There's a shiver of mortality in the air.
You draw the blinds. You need darkness.
You enter the elevator on the thirty-first floor of an office
　　building in midtown Manhattan.
"How was the Biennial?" "Repulsive."
There is the easy laugh of men who did their tour of Vietnam
　　together and still wake up screaming some mornings.
False dawn. The Milky Way like a pilgrimage of clouds.
"The first thing you see are three dozen mattresses hanging from
　　the ceiling smeared with cake."
"I heard there was a rubber puddle of *faux* vomit." "No, that was
　　the last Biennial."
The first man laughs. He's a lucky guy. On the twenty-first
　　floor he steps off the elevator
And into Japan, where he lives on a German salary with a
　　Japanese wife, a French cook, and an English education.
The second man is feeling bitter. He wishes he could feel neutral
　　in the face of cultural degradation.
He knows that the makers of jeremiads are universally regarded as
　　bores, but he can't help himself.
The decline of our culture weighs heavily on his mind.
He gets off on the mysterious fifth floor, about which much has
　　been written but little is known,
Leaving you alone with your thoughts, which are about your love of
　　language
As manifest in such words as *eyewear*, such phrases as *for medicinal
　　purposes* (spoken always by a cleric as he takes out
A flask of brandy from the desk drawer), such screamers as *Stop me
　　before I kill again*.

Every dream is an example of something, an elevator going in one
    direction only,
Speeding up as it descends, with a neon sign on one of the walls
Flashing the letters of the word *WAR* one at a time backwards.

TIMES SQUARE

His homage to the square was a cube of yellow light.
People lived in squares. J. said, Why don't we?
The light turned red. The machine took the call.
But would she call back? The lines were drawn
And were blue, like a wave hurling the ship,
But she and he could never agree about the frequency
Or the constancy of human desire, no matter what
Their biologist friend said, just back from Périgord,
Where she had seen the caves and was now convinced
That the first words spoken by a man were a poem.
All poems were love songs in the marriage chamber.
Art preceded commerce. Well, maybe. But not here,
Where all roads lead to New Jersey. The curved lips
Do not smile. And the arc of their friendship was like
An impromptu meeting on a bridge connecting two ideas
As large as Manhattan and the rest of the United States.

But it turned out to be a decent deal for the women.
The mirror. She read bodice rippers for a living
Hysterical phone call. The husband went to New Jersey
Black lace visible under her dress-for-success suit
When I worked at 444 Madison Avenue one Friday night
Man's a toilet-trained ape, everywhere in chains,
And the urologist holding a test tube to the light
Had beauty in his eyes. It was a warm January evening.
Somehow she ripped his jacket at the party.
What was that photographer doing? But she wanted it
When this avenue was a synonym for advertising.
The creative director was willing to take it up
If it was a question of humming in the elevator
With her mother who screamed at her for half an hour
Don't go. The need to develop new euphemisms for snow
No one's job is safe, and neither is sex
Comic books read by convicts. The polls were faked,
Were not, and the third drink didn't taste as good
Afterwards. Yellow was the color. A slow curve.

THE THEORY
OF THE LEISURE CLASSES

❧

In theory the sky was gray all that winter in London: no central
heating, a constant drizzle, your feet were constantly cold.
In practice it was the same old overheated New York City apartment
—but once you went outside, how near the sky, how blue.

In theory a man watching as a woman dresses, slowly, slowly, for the
benefit of his gaze, is a man to be envied.
In practice he needs a shave.

In theory a man choosing among three women—his past wife, his
future wife, and his current mistress—chooses the mistress.
In practice he is choosing among the daughters of King Lear.

In theory the revolver in the desk drawer was not meant to be used—
it was a prop in a play, to be brandished once or twice by the
hero in a fit of temperament.
In practice the newlyweds soon discovered the limits of their tolerance
for each other's quirks.

In theory it was a trip to the places on the postage stamps in the
collection I had as a boy: Magyar Poste, Československo,
Jugoslavia, Deutsches Reich, Österreich.
In practice it was the experience of examining a 1957 Duke Snider
baseball card fifteen years later, and noticing how young Snider
looked. He hit forty home runs that season, the Dodgers' last in
Brooklyn.

In theory she was the right woman at the wrong airport. It was the
first time he had seen her without her makeup.

In practice she wears flats and never comes into Manhattan without
having stockings on. Watching her walk back and forth back and
forth in front of him, the auburn-haired man in the dark shirt and
tie calculates the exact relation of danger to desire.

In theory the passengers are irate. "You are inept," an owlish-looking
gentleman hooted at a red-faced customer service agent. Two cops
turn up and the unattended shoe box in the TWA ticket area
becomes the object of lively discussion. Then the announcement
is made. Everyone has to clear the area—it's a real live bomb scare,
folks.
In practice you take a cab into the city and notice for the first time the
little shopfront at Lexington Avenue and 94th Street: Chao's
Laundry. Remove the apostrophe and you arrive at your chosen
destination. The adrenaline automatically starts to flow.

In theory the voice of authority is never heard—the word unspoken is
what commands us.
In practice I was having lunch with an executive in the publishing
industry. He said that success in management meant "having
not only the responsibility but also the authority." Later I heard
the same phrase from the general manager of the San Francisco
Giants and from a guy I know in middle management in
Rochester. I figured it must be true.

In theory a man does his best work under the pressure of deadlines
and production schedules.
In practice a man does his best work on a beach in Bermuda, on an
exceptionally clear October day, followed by rum swizzles at
sundown and a little night reading.

In theory the woman was absent.
In practice every inch of the canvas implicated her in the man's idle
fantasies of leisure and success.

PART III

❧

VALENTINE PLACE

[a sequence]

❧

Mother was born today. I traveled back to watch her
In the school play, crying because her mother wasn't there.
There was always a crisis in the tailor shop in Vienna.
Father smoked cigars. What he liked about his life was
The chance to do the same thing twice—to lose the lady
A second time, flee from Europe, and live in a grand hotel,
Looking sharp in a tuxedo among the gambling tables.
If childhood is a foreign country, his had armed guards
At the barbed-wire border. "Don't you remember me,"
The lady asked plaintively. He shook his head no, grinning
Like a soldier before combat, "But I'm willing to learn."
Sometimes the memory of her face was all that kept him going.
He had to see her again. It didn't matter where or when.
They would go to Coney Island, eat hot dogs, be American.
America was young then, naïve, brash, confident.
The immigrants were pouring in: new blood, old guts.
And when the market crashed, and banks started failing,
My old man gave me a piece of advice that I've never
Forgotten, though I never did manage to follow it.
Get the money. Cut your losses. Always look your partner
In the eye, except when kissing her warm red lips,
Drunk on her aroma, surprised to be alive.

What a life: hospitals and airports, clocks in corridors,
Mother asleep in the next room, and Dad waking up to piss,
Knocking over the glass of water and the vial of pills
On the night table. It took him all these years
To learn that America hated eggheads and queers,
And death was everywhere, a foreign language
Spoken by everybody but him: the old people obsessed
With their money, and the predatory brokers
In their strip-mall offices, making steeples
Out of their hands. America was New York, but New York
Was moving South, going fast, reaching Miami in 1979,
The year marijuana use reached an all-time high
In high schools; he read about it in the national edition
Of today's *Times*. Today he was with the two people
He loved the best in all the world, and the level
Of hysteria, always high, was rising in the living room.
Why was it so hard to make them happy? The party
Was over twelve years ago, yet only now did he realize it
And weep, driving with his friend from Coral Gables
In her big red Buick, with Frank Sinatra on the tape deck
And the Biltmore Hotel out the window. These palm trees
Made him happy. They were Miami when life was real.

THIRD ACT

❧

Too much coffee. Her mind was racing. Relief of tension:
Was fucking no more than this? Love no nobler than parking?
"He specialized in giving her hell." She wanted him
Anyway. Something other than the law of mimetic desire
("I want you because she does") was at work. She had watched
Enough movies to understand: Vietnam was the product
Of bad grass, a paranoid trip on the IRT, and the garbage
Was growing, a living organism like the monster
In a Japanese movie, circa 1954. What a strange wonderful island
America was, a monument to impermanence and ocean foam.
Old people lived there, arguing noisily in slow elevators
About mothers in nursing homes, fathers in graves,
Children with knives in the school cafeteria—
I need a drink. "How they could make a six-part documentary
About the Sixties, and never mention the pill,
I don't understand," she said. "I have a better sense of humor
Than you do," said her seven-year-old son, "because I'm more
Serious than you are." He was right. In the fresh green breast
Of the new world, he had sought a compliant nipple. In time
The darkness would overcome him, sweet as the sweat of sex.
"I love you," he lied. "I love you, too," she replied,
Waking beside him in the morning, scaring him with her love.

❧

You could have an affair with her but you
Could never marry her. She was the Sarah Lawrence sophomore
Who met him at the station wearing a fur coat
And nothing underneath. She was a dancer.
She liked staying in the air. He liked watching her
Land. Then she changed her hairstyle. Then she changed
Her name. She knew she wanted a career
In TV news, a personal trainer, a husband,
And a baby in that order. Something
Had to give and deep down he always knew he was
Expendable. Still it came as a shock when she
Sent his few belongings back to him in a box
Without a note. He missed her but he
Would get over that. He was a professional,
And would do as they asked, would go where he was sent.
So he lived alone in this bewildering city, where they spoke
A medley of languages not his own. He had come here to be
Anonymous, with forged identity papers, vague instructions,
And only a few photographs to torture himself with.
It dawned on him that he had no proof of his actual existence.
The thought exhilarated him, as a TV weatherman is exhilarated
By a major blizzard, with gale-force winds knocking down
Power lines in shore towns all along the coast.

FIFTH AMENDMENT

❦

The fear of perjuring herself turned into a tacit
Admission of her guilt. Yet she had the skill
And the luck to elude her implacable pursuers.
God was everywhere like a faceless guard in a gallery.
Death was last seen in the auction room, looking worried.
She hadn't seen him leave. She narrowly avoided him
Walking past the hard hats eating lunch. Which one was he?
She felt like one of those women you sometimes see
Crying in a hotel lobby. But he couldn't figure her out.
She wrote him a letter saying, "Please don't phone me,"
Meaning, "Please phone me." And there were times when she
Refused to speak at all. Would this be one of them?
On went the makeup and the accessories. Her time was now,
And he could no more share her future than she
Could go to college with him twenty years ago.
She would have had a tremendous crush on him
Back then, with his scarf flying in the wind like
The National League pennant flying over Ebbets Field
In Brooklyn, borough of churches, with the pigeons on the sill
And the soprano's trill echoing in the alley.

DAVID LEHMAN

SIXTH SENSE

❧

Something told him she was near. In the same room,
Even. Wearing the blue polka-dot dress he'd given her,
With the pearl choker and the sapphire earrings,
Holding a Kir Royale. He looked at her left hand.
No ring. And knew he had to get out of there
Fast, before one of them did something irrevocable,
Like the time she slapped his face in the bus
And he wasn't sure why, or the day they stood
In front of the dress-shop window, and when
She said she liked the yellow kimono he went
And bought it on the spot. What an amazing day
That was. Everyone he met that day was someone
He had known before, a decade ago or more,
And the statue of Alice the gigantic girl
In Central Park turned out to be his sister
When they were small. Mama was in the kitchen
Waiting for the phone to ring, and Daddy was still
On the road, checking the rearview mirror
In the old green Chevrolet, when the hurricane hit.
One of the other men drowned that night, but Daddy
Came back safely, with gifts for all the kids
If they agreed to go to sleep and dream of him.

SEVENTH HEAVEN

After he left, she thought about him every day
The way President Kennedy's name turned up
In the paper, after the assassination, every day
For more than a hundred days, until one day it stopped—
And life was real again. The actor playing Lee Harvey Oswald
Returns to play Beethoven, and the New York native
Returns to the city enraptured with the sight
Of fire escapes and water towers, the skyline observed
From Brooklyn Heights or the Triborough Bridge
As the taxi heads to the airport. How happy she was.
He wanted her as much as she wanted him.
The knowledge was bliss, though it terrified them both.
It was windy enough for her to do artful things
With her scarf in the car. If it was a conspiracy,
Everyone was in on it, including the driver,
A massage therapist who moonlights on Wall Street,
Which begins in a graveyard and ends in a river.
She was prepared to impersonate his wife
Even if that meant she would have to marry him.

EIGHTH WONDER

❧

No gentle way to break the news: you turn on the TV
And see the rocket's red glare: the capsule explodes,
The astronauts tumble down, and the anchorpeople
Look solemn, saying, "The nation grieves tonight."
Sure it does, Buster, snorted the man with the pencil mustache,
Lying in the shabby, unmade bed in this most mediocre
Of motels in New Mexico. When did we stop believing that life
Was real? Was it when we let these puppets do the living for us,
As if the esthetic credo of the French Symbolists
Could somehow work for us today? The questions were meant
To be ignored, which made them definitively rhetorical, but she,
His first wife, insisted on asking them anyway. She shared
His love of noble gestures and hopeless causes
Such as the idea of romantic love in a pragmatic era
When the macrostructure no longer values that unit
Of individual gratification. There was a time, not very long ago,
When it didn't seem that way. It was the age of innocence
In a double sense, and we must have needed it badly, or else
We'd have never grown up to regret the spoiling of the planet,
The shrinking of the garden, near the graves where children play.

NINTH INNING

❧

He woke up in New York City on Valentine's Day,
Speeding. The body in the booth next to his was still warm,
Was gone. He had bought her a sweater, a box of chocolate
Said her life wasn't working he looked stricken she said
You're all bent out of shape, accusingly, and when he
She went from being an Ivy League professor of French
To an illustrator for a slick midtown magazine
They agreed it was his fault. But for now they needed
To sharpen to a point like a pencil the way
The Empire State Building does. What I really want to say
To you, my love, is a whisper on the rooftop lost in the wind
And you turn to me with your rally cap on backwards rooting
For a big inning, the bases loaded, our best slugger up
And no one out, but it doesn't work that way. Like the time
Kirk Gibson hit the homer off Dennis Eckersley to win the game:
It doesn't happen like that in fiction. In fiction, we are
On a train, listening to a storyteller about to reach the climax
Of his tale as the train pulls into Minsk, his stop. That's
My stop, he says, stepping off the train, confounding us who
Can't get off it. "You can't leave without telling us the end,"
We say, but he is already on the platform, grinning.
"End?" he says. "It was only the beginning."

TENTH COMMANDMENT

The woman said yes she would go to Australia with him
Unless he heard wrong and she said Argentina
Where they could learn the tango and pursue the widows
Of Nazi war criminals unrepentant to the end.
But no, she said Australia. She'd been born in New Zealand.
The difference between the two places was the difference
Between a hamburger and a chocolate malted, she said.
In the candy store across from the elementary school,
They planned their tryst. She said Australia, which meant
She was willing to go to bed with him, and this
Was before her husband's coronary
At a time when a woman didn't take off her underpants
If she didn't like you. She said Australia,
And he saw last summer's seashell collection
In a plastic bag on a shelf in the mud room
With last summer's sand. The cycle of sexual captivity
Beginning in romance and ending in adultery
Was now in the late middle phases, the way America
Had gone from barbarism to amnesia without
A period of high decadence, which meant something,
But what? A raft on the rapids? The violinist
At the gate? Oh, absolute is the law of biology.
For the pornography seminar, what should she wear?

ELEVENTH HOUR

❧

The bloom was off the economic recovery.
"I just want to know one thing," she said.
What was that one thing? He'll never know,
Because at just that moment he heard the sound
Of broken glass in the bathroom, and when he got there,
It was dark. His hand went to the wall
But the switch wasn't where it was supposed to be
Which felt like déjà vu. And then she was gone.
And now he knew how it felt to stand
On the local platform as the express whizzes by
With people chatting in a dialect
Of English he couldn't understand, because his English
Was current as of 1968 and no one speaks that way except
In certain books. So the hours spent in vain
Were minutes blown up into comic-book balloons full
Of Keats's odes. "Goodbye, kid." Tears streamed down
The boy's face. It was a great feeling,
Like the feeling you get when you throw things away
After a funeral: clean and empty in the morning dark.
There was no time for locker-room oratory.
They knew they were facing a do-or-die situation,
With their backs to the wall, and no tomorrow.

TWELFTH NIGHT

❧

His first infidelity was a mistake, but not as big
As her false pregnancy. Later, the boy found out
He was born three months earlier than the date
On his birth certificate. Had he been trapped
In a net, like a moth mistaken for a butterfly?
And why did she—what was in it for her?
It took him all this time to figure it out.
The barroom boast, "I never had to pay for it,"
Is bogus if marriage is a religious institution
On the operating model of a nineteenth-century factory.
On the other hand, women's lot was no worse then
Than it is now. The division of labor made sense
In theories developed by college boys in jeans
Who grasped the logic their fathers had used
To seduce women and deceive themselves.
The pattern repeats itself, the same events
In a different order obeying the conventions of
A popular genre. Winter on a desolate beach. Spring
While there's snow still on the balcony and,
In the window, a plane flies over the warehouse.
The panic is gone. But the pain remains. And the apple,
The knife, and the honey are months away.

LAST WORDS

"Enough." "No, more." "Not me," he said, closing the door,
Walking away from the blaze in the bedroom behind him.
"I'm going straight." He could barely see. The sun was blinding.
Yet he knew they would come for him—it was only a matter
Of time. "Mama," he called, though the personage thus named
Was dead, and had been dead for decades, an ocean away,
In another city, another land. A stenographer was on hand
To record his last words. "I don't need a priest," he said.
Then the lights went out. It was the old familiar thrill
Of homesickness all over again. The slow earth churned on
And the money—the money was gone. Gone like *that* (he snapped
His fingers). Gone forever. And so, after the longest delay
In the history of the Trans-Siberian Express, the landscape
Began to rumble forward, just as the old fool said it would.
Europe was still the biggest bloody thing in North America.
There were no more plans. They had all turned into hospitals.
And there was nothing left to eat or smoke. A dream of tomorrow,
A prayer to an absent deity, what difference did it make?
He couldn't remember how he got here or who he was,
Only that he was still alive—that was the miraculous part,
And nothing she did would change his mind. She licked her lips.
"More," he said, liking the sound. "More, more, more!"

PART IV

WHO SHE WAS

❧

She loved jumping on the trampoline.
Her nickname was Monkey.
She slipped her tongue in his mouth when they kissed.

She had a job in publishing. It was what
she most wanted after she got out of Vassar. The first
manuscript she acquired was *The Heidegger Cookbook,*
so you can imagine how her career took off from there.

She started liking sex soon after her husband left her.
He came back weekends and complied
with her bedtime wishes. A lawyer.
What did you expect? A Peace Corps
volunteer who went on to become
the editor of *Envy: The Magazine for You*?

Where did her anger come from? He wasn't sure
but it was how he knew she loved him.

It was heartbreaking to learn that they
had both married other people. "What is the most
heartbreaking thing you can think of?"
he asked. Her list included the dawn,
Vassar graduation, and the city
of Paris, which she described in vivid prose
before she set foot in France. It was
the one infallible rule she used
to write her acclaimed series of travel guidebooks.

He realized why he married her:
so he wouldn't have to think about her,
or about sex, or about other women: the hours
they consumed like crossword puzzles
and chocolate-covered cherries.

She said the most obvious things
but she said them well.

She tried to impress people but kept blundering
as when she attributed the phrase "Make It New"
to William Carlos Williams.

She had the soul of a stranger.
There were things that she loved besides herself—
flowers, poems.

She was obsessed with the difficulty
of finding good nectarines in New York City.
They cost an arm and a leg and were mealy.

She said something critical
He flew off the handle
She asked, "Are you saying it's over?"
He said Fuck you
She said Fuck you and told him to leave
All right, he said, I'm leaving
if that's the way you want it
and if you want to know
where I am, I'm in Palm Springs
fucking Lana Turner
as Frank Sinatra put it to Ava Gardner
who was in her bathtub at the time
it was 1952

She got so depressed she stayed in her room
all day. At least that way she would stay
out of trouble. Her job kept her sedentary.
The only exercise she got was fixing a sandwich
and writing dialogue for a man and a woman
while one is packing a suitcase: "What are you
doing?" "What does it look like I'm doing?"

It rained all day, converting a September morning
into a November afternoon. The speed
of thinking was faster than the speed of light.
"How's your ex-wife?"
"She's divorced, too," he replied.
"That's what we have in common."

He had the odd habit of smiling when he was tense.
This made him a lousy poker player but won her sympathy.
She liked his bohemian life. Or didn't really
but said she did. The joy went out of his eyes
but the smile stayed on his face
having nowhere else to go. God's image
was shaving in the mirror, feeling like hell,
missing her, wondering who she was.

INFIDELITY

❧

1.

She went to his head like a double martini at a bar
Where gangsters gather after a hit. She wanted his baby.
They sat at a corner table, quarreling about money,
When the full force of her passion hit him at last.

He couldn't get enough of her. He wanted her
And would always want her, though his daydreams implied
A future without her. Theirs would be a civilized affair;
They would part, go home, and divorce their spouses

On the appointed day. They were just using each other,
Afraid of losing each other, but that didn't matter.
This was their chance to be young again forever,

And he knew he would never forget her fragrance
Or the scent of death in the hotel room full of flowers,
Her dress in the closet, as he stepped in the door.

2.

Why couldn't she be happy with what they had?
Everyone recommended it: her lawyer, his bartender,
Her mother, his priest. He kissed her hard
On the mouth, then stood there with a goofy grin

While she put her hand in his pants, and he
Couldn't resist her, or bear to look at her later,

And she—she thought he had some fucking nerve
To treat her like that, ignoring her at the party,

And never introducing her to his friends. Who did he
Think he was? She called him up to say she loved him
And wondered why he was living with this pallid woman

Who answered the phone. Out of what archaic notion
Of honor, or gratitude for kindnesses and kisses past,
Long past? "You'll be happier loving me," she said.

3.

She wanted to write a novel. He gave her *Madame Bovary,*
Anna Karenina, and Nabokov's *King, Queen, Knave*. In each
The heroine dies, she noticed. She called him up to say
Love is a verb and I want you inside me, baby. Had he

Ever loved her? Would he ever love her again? And then
Came the anxiety, whose circumference was nowhere,
And depression, when cause and effect got all mixed up
In her brain: she'd feel guilty so she'd get a ticket

For speeding. When she called him to tell him off,
She meant to say she loved him, because he was
The American in this British novel: tight-lipped, hungover,

Whose wife won't sleep with him and whose mistress
Hangs up on him, making him feel guilty, because
Why couldn't he be happy with what they had?

THE PLEASURE PRINCIPLE

Ten years later he was still sleeping
With one woman while dreaming of another
With his eyes wide open. *I'm not your mother,*
She said. *I'm not out to smother you.* In some ways
He struck her as naïve. On some days
She felt she had betrayed herself for him.

Yes, she confessed. She was keeping
A journal, planning to blackmail him.
But she was not just the product of his desire for her.
She was *not* a victim.
His mind was the most masculine part of him,
She told him, hating herself for loving him.

Her kisses beguiled him, though her anger terrorized him,
And he promised her anything if only she'd stop phoning him
At two forty-five in the morning, because he missed her
Just as she predicted, now that he was through with her
And she was through with him. It drove him
Wild, seeing her from across the room like this, watching her

Depart, in the white silk blouse she was wearing for him
For the first and last time. *Do it,* she hissed.
They kissed; his kisses loosened her tongue.
She told him she was mad about him
And would prove it to him, if he let her.
That's what he liked about her. She kept him young.

TOWARD A DEFINITION
OF LOVE

❦

1.

Another time they were making love. "It's even better
When you help," she said. That was the second thing
He liked about her: she had memorized hours
Of movie dialogue, as if their life together
In the close apartment, with the street noise,
The crank calls, and the sinister next-door neighbor,
Consisted of roles to be played with panache,
If possible, and with a song in her heart. Was she lying
When she told him she loved him? Or was she
The nude in his bed with her back to him
As if he were a painter in Paris in 1870
And she were a model in Brooklyn in 1992,
And what separated them was a painted ocean
Representing the unbridgeable distance between them,
As between age and youth, Europe and America?
A condition of their romance was its impossibility—
She would have panicked if he had proposed,
Because love was passion consuming itself
Like a flickering cigarette, an ember in an ashtray.

2.

When she went back to sleep, he thought about her
Some more, and what they had done the night before:
Something holy, but with awful consequences,
Like a revolution about to enter its reign of terror.

DAVID LEHMAN

In the movie, he was the jilted soldier ("don't you still
Love me?") or the Scandinavian philosopher ("he wondered
Why he had to give her up"). But their lines so truly parallel
Though infinite could never meet, and there was no use
Arguing against the despair that had wakened his longing
For her, now that she was gone. There was no way
To make it last, to prolong a moment of such pleasure,
Sweet and intense, that Faust would have bargained away
His soul for it. In public they acted married. One day
She left. She phoned from the road. A morning of tears
In honor of the first morning he had woken up beside her
With the shades rattling in the window, and the rays
Of light seeping weakly into the room, and the noise
Of the kids playing with a ball in the gutter.

YOUNG DEATH

The sky was the color of coffee in an all-night truck stop
Where guys go who have just left their wives
You put a quarter in the jukebox and nothing comes out
He checks his wrist, it is three in the morning
Yet when he looks up, the people are different
The clock on the wall says it's three the next afternoon
And somebody else's kids in the booth next to his
Were playing childhood, a game, when he heard them crying
Daddy, daddy, we were afraid you wouldn't find us
You know a woman loves you when she wants to have your baby

The subject was average height average weight
With a wife who wanted a divorce
And a mistress who could have been her identical twin
And he was intoxicated with his own thoughts
Driving from one highway to the next, smoking
To avoid going to sleep at the wheel
And waking up at the diner, where she was wearing
A nurse's white uniform, bearing a syringe on a tray

And he loved her because she was as selfish as he
As intoxicated with her own thoughts, and unable to see
Her image except in the innermost coat
Of his eyeball, continuous with the optic nerve.
Loving her was like crawling on his belly across the border
Into the forest of human history
After a major fire had nearly wiped it out.
They left the scene of the crime together, her hand in his,
Yet in her dream she was alone, carrying their baby, a boy,
And a few years later he's in center field, a tall skinny kid

DAVID LEHMAN

Who could never please his father, no matter what he did,
Until he became his father, ran away from home—
And he will always be a stranger in this place
Carrying a new passport, wearing a different face

Some place not too far away, a little out of the ordinary
But not by much, ringed with hills an easy drive from the valley
On dirt roads lined with mom-and-pop refreshment stands,
The kind of place where they didn't ask questions
And you could get a job washing dishes in some dive
Keeping your eyes open and your wits about you
When other strangers arrived, one at a time, sleepless men
Who had ditched their trucks and hitched into town
With a suitcase and a good sense of direction,
And after a while women, too, began to arrive,
And the property values shot up, and so did the taxes.
A sip of the day's first martini: heaven.

The couple in the toy store, who have just committed adultery,
Are looking for something to buy for her son
And something to buy for his daughter,
And the man's name is Death. Young Death.

Young Death woke up with the world's worst hangover.
He was a hustler. A regular guy. The type
Who drinks alone and sits quietly at the bar. In short,
He fit the profile of the lone assassin perfectly,
Yet was surprised when he landed the part.
The woman in the torn nightgown waiting for him upstairs
Was in on the plot, as were the neighbors and the cops
On his tail, closing in. He knew the back alleys of this city
And had escaped twice already. Would he luck out again?
Yes, for he was Young Death, whose middle name was Boy—

And she was the woman of his dreams, the mother of his child,
His split end, his tight end, his wide receiver,
And she wants more
Wants it now, wants it fast, faster than ever before,
Like the sound of her heart in his ear. She was a real ball-buster.

She was intoxicated with her thoughts
Littering the ground like red and yellow leaves,
And the little boy who walked sometimes beside them
Would pick up the leaves and paste them back on the branches,
And this was their American dream: the pursuit of happiness.
They thought they were moving toward it and not just away from
The stubborn grass growing in sidewalk cracks:
No natural religion, but they were born for loneliness,
No natural laws, and no real difference between freedom and chaos,
Nothing besides the conviction that they were blessed

O America land of the same mistake twice—

The flickering lamp lighting up that tiny portion of sky
Which was to be their lot, stretching out to infinity.
You had to forgive them. It may have been a sin
But you could tell that they did it out of passion
And you didn't have the heart to condemn them.

The hero fell for the flashy dame, and cried when he lost her.
The game was over. He married the pretty brunette,
And fate is kind to the young couple, blessing them
With a pair of cute kids two jobs and a backyard barbecue
Until the day he drives off in his Ford, a gray morning.
He didn't say a word, just turned on the radio
And sang along with the crooners. No one ever heard from him again.
That man was living the dream, and if a bum steer
Took him south instead of west, it didn't change a thing.
He said he loved her, wanting to sleep with her,

DAVID LEHMAN

And now he can't find her, so he is driving
Past necking couples wishing they were older, leaving
Without more possessions than he can fit in his car.
The most American thing he can think of is leaving,
Never felt as free as when he was in motion,
Leaving without knowing where he was going,
Without saying goodbye, no notes, no explanations.
The high windows were watching every move he was making.
The calendar's pages fluttered in the wind.

ON THE RUN

❧

"Too late," said Uncle Alvin, checking his watch.
He was supposed to take the boy to the funeral,
Little suspecting it would be his own. *Too late*:
The killing words. " 'But, my friend, we have come
Too late,' said the hero." The textbook salesman
In the motel room can hear the words echo
In his ear, and wonders what they mean in *his* case:
Has he left something undone? Neglected someone
He should have loved? More than likely. Yet
Even at twenty-eight, years before the age of regret,
He had already heard the words. It was too late
To assemble the birds as he had pictured them
One spring morning. Too late to marry the girl
And sire numerous offspring in bohemian splendor.
Too late for anything but life on the run, life
As he was living it, in motels and rental cars,
Running away from something, though not sure what,
Running in place, to keep up with the others,
In pursuit of the ring rolling down the street
Or to escape into the glory of an unknown destiny.
Running into enemy territory, as fast as a boy.

BOY WITH RED HAIR

❦

1.

The boy was shy. He was quietly bored in the dark house but too nice
    to say so.

One afternoon at three-thirty the mother didn't show up and the boy
    had to take a taxi from school to house. He was furious with her.
    "He was so angry he reminded me of you," the mother told her
    ex-husband.

I guess I inherit my absentmindedness from her, said the boy.
He was old-fashioned, with freckles and red hair,
and when they drove through a tollbooth
the man at the tollbooth would say, "Hi, Red."

The boy and his grandfather had several things in common.
Both were soft-spoken, sincere hypochondriacs.
Their favorite fruits were strawberries in summer
and pears in fall.

A parrot alighted on the boy's shoulder.
See, the cage's door was wide open the whole time.
Later, the boy made eye contact
with a butterfly settling on his shoe.

The boy was slow in the bathroom, thinking
while brushing his teeth.
What was he thinking about?
"Did you know Jack Nicholson played a killer
in *Cry Baby Killer,* his first movie?"

Hours later he couldn't reconstruct the thought processes that had
led to this moment.

2.

The boy put his yellow-and-brown-checked pajama bottoms
around his head and became Invulnerable Man.
Swinging himself around,
he knocked down a vase, which crashed.
And then he got quiet, very quiet.

The boy had a respect for silence.
He didn't say one word more than was strictly necessary.
On the phone he would say *uh-huh* and *yes* and little else.

He liked long car trips. His father asked,
What would you paint—the clouds
or the trees—if you were a painter?
The boy thought for what seemed like a long time.
He thought it would be difficult to paint the clouds.
Ladders weren't long enough.

3.

That night he slept in the Château d'If.

"Do not underestimate me," said the German commandant.
"From this prison there is no escape."
The boy had heard these words before. He knew what came next.
The commandant needed to make an example of somebody.
He would pick a prisoner at random and have him hanged.
This would frighten the others,

DAVID LEHMAN

and the hunger strike would be over.
In prison there was plenty of time to imagine the scene.

In prison there was time to waste, wondering why he was there,
making appeals, pleading for a hearing,
when he should have been playing on the porch
listening to the birds singing
or digging a tunnel from his bed
to the mad priest's cell, substituting
his body for the dead man's in the shroud
after memorizing the map of his secret treasure,
ready to return to life, to swim all the way
to Paris if necessary, a nobleman in a cape,
ready to exact his revenge.

FLASHBACK

❧

The lonely boy in the blue snowsuit playing
With the dog that didn't exist
In the yard of the house that hadn't yet been built
Was the older brother I never had, and he was
Carving a snow palace guarded by soldiers and stone lions
Where violins played waltzes from the Vienna woods
While in the big bay window in the living room
You could see the mouths of his parents moving
And though you couldn't hear the words
You knew a divorce was in the cards, and then you see
A close-up of the mother's face and suddenly
You can tell what she will look like in twenty years
And what she looked like twenty years ago.
The boy vanishes. It continues to snow.

THE END OF THE AFFAIR

❧

1.

It may have been what she wanted all along:
An episode in a foreign film, Swedish or French,
Where the laconic man and woman in the hotel lobby
Have their last chance to act nobly, stoically,
Before they are separated by the fortunes of war,
And each forgives the other, and neither is to blame.

Or it may have been what she wanted all along:
The intoxication of paranoia, where the suspicion is mutual,
And she doesn't know what he does for a living,
And he knows that her last two lovers died violent deaths.
It was like the rush of inspiration that only a nervous breakdown
Can give you: she looked at the roses and burst into tears.

2.

It was as if she had brewed a supremely powerful pot of coffee
For breakfast, and he watched as it transported her
To Paris and the smell of bakeries in May, and she watched
As he went back to the day he noticed something different
About his wife, her hair or a new silk scarf she was wearing,
That made him realize she was having an affair. It was almost

Like being inside a snow-filled paperweight, which someone shakes:
It was snowing, he won't forget, and she told him
He made her feel beautiful in the snow, and what he wanted

Was what he thought he wanted—delight in the body
Sleeping next to his, the curve of her back, the barrette
That fell out of her hair as she slept.

DUTCH INTERIOR

❧

He liked the late-afternoon light as it dimmed
In the living room, and wouldn't switch on
The electric lights until past eight o'clock.
His wife complained, called him cheerless, but
It wasn't a case of melancholy; he just liked
The way things looked in air growing darker
So gradually and imperceptibly that it seemed
The very element in which we live. Every man
And woman deserves one true moment of greatness
And this was his, this Dutch interior, entered
And possessed, so tranquil and yet so busy
With details: the couple's shed clothes scattered
On the backs of armchairs, the dog chasing a shoe,
The wide-open window, the late-afternoon light.

Grateful acknowledgment is made to the editors of the magazines in which these poems first appeared:

American Letters & Commentary: "The Pleasure Principle"
American Poetry Review: "Breeze Marine," "The Choice," "Madison Avenue," "Times Square"
Antioch Review: "First Lines," "Third Act" [*as* "Guilt Trip"]
Boulevard: "The Role Model," "The Secret Life," "The Theory of the Leisure Classes"
Boston Phoenix: "Flashback," "Fourth Estate"
Colorado Review: "Young Death"
The Forward: "A Little History"
The Gettysburg Review: "The Public Sector"
Harvard Magazine: "Dutch Interior," "Seventh Heaven"
Michigan Quarterly Review: "On the Nature of Desire," "Toward a Definition of Love"
New American Writing: "1967," "The Visit"
The New Republic: "Dark Passage," "Last Words," "Under the Influence"
The New Yorker: "The End of the Affair," "On the Run," "Sixth Sense," "Stages on Life's Way," "Who She Was"
The Paris Review: "Boy with Red Hair," "Eighth Wonder" [*as* "Shock Therapy"], "Infidelity," "Sexism," "Wedding Song," "The World Trade Center"
Ploughshares: "Fifth Amendment," "Ninth Inning," "Tenth Commandment," "Eleventh Hour," "Twelfth Night"
The Stud Duck: "The World Trade Center"
Virginia Quarterly Review: "The Drowning," "Second Thoughts"
Western Humanities Review: "The Interruption"

The author would like to thank the Lila Wallace–Reader's Digest Fund for a three-year writer's award, the Guggenheim Foundation for a fellowship grant, and the Ingram Merrill Foundation for an award in poetry. Without their generous support this book could not have been written.